The Philadelphia METALS

About the Poet

Wendy Ruthroff was born in Yorkshire, England. She spent her riper years abroad, first in France and later in the U.S.A. She now lives in Devon, England. She has an M.A. in Creative Writing. She has a son and three daughters.

She is an experienced performer and her poetry has been published in the following anthologies:

No Time to Retire (1991), Stride Publications
Virago New Poets (1993), Virago Press Ltd
The Barnet Poetry Anthology (1995), Barnet Borough Arts Council
Her Mind's Eye (1996), Pyramid Press
The Three Disgraces (1996)
Sean's House (1996), White Box Publications, Exeter
Etc Dreams (1997), Spineless Press
"formally quite messy ..." (1997), Flarestack, Redditch Library Poetry
        Competition

This, her first collection, *The Philadelphia Metals – a poem sequence*, was first published by Flarestack in 1997.

Poet's royalties will be donated to the Green Gulch Farm Zen Center.

From the Poet

These poems came as a gift to me, inspired by twisted wire artifacts mostly made from urban detritus. They had been found in a skip in the USA and found their way into a museum. It was from black and white prints that their power reached out to me in England. These poems were born as a result of that open and intimate relationship.

I acknowledge and heartily thank Selima Hill (writer of and inspirer of poetry), Gillian Allnutt, who gave the sequence a prize, and Charles Johnson, who subsequently published it in 1997. I give deep appreciation to Mitchell Ginsberg for the chance to see these poems republished – an unexpected excitement in my old age. Thanks to Mark Øvland for the emails – without him, nothing.

Wendy Ruthroff
Totnes, Devon, UK
March 2, 2012

The Philadelphia METALS

a poem sequence

First US Edition

Wendy Authroff

Wisdom Moon Publishing

THE PHILADELPHIA METALS
A POEM SEQUENCE
(First U.S. Edition)

Copyright © 2012 Wisdom Moon Publishing LLC

All rights reserved. Tous droits réservés.

Published by Wisdom Moon Publishing LLC
San Diego, CA, USA

Wisdom Moon™, the Wisdom Moon logo™, *Wisdom Moon Publishing*™, and *WMP*™
are trademarks of Wisdom Moon Publishing LLC.

Photograph of Wendy Ruthroff by John Pollex.

ISBN 978-1-938459-02-3 (softcover, alk. paper)
ISBN 978-1-938459-05-4 (eBook)

9 8 7 6 5 4 3 2 1

The Philadelphia METALS

Entry 1 from the Diary of Noemi/e\n
After Earth Time cosine 12.

Today I have started something that must lead
to an established compatibility programme.
We've exchanged code, we're both E and N
but he's ungalvanised – so sexy.
I daren't ask if his strokes were forward or backward.
I just know he must have universal valency.
Proof positive – all my test spots were molten.
Could it be too soon after that attack
of corrosion type Z? No. Orwen will be
the very thing for my Post-rust crumbles.
What a construction – big and solid,
I love it.
I'm ready for every twisted metre and knew it
the moment my silver bands tightened.
Vicious! I don't care if it unravels me.
I'm going to have Orwen.
It's the size of him that's irresistible.

Roll on period 13. See you, Orwen,
Post-rust Rehabilitation Lot One.

Entry 2. AET (After Earth Time)
cosine 14. Shortly after the happy event.

Some say, because Orwen and I have activated FBR
(Full Blown Rust), our first connection produced
Little Injun – that's what I WANTED to call him –
but Orwen doesn't like the name.
At last we've agreed on the nickname Li.
Now, it's his smallness that bothers us.
We've consulted the gene brain.
He says the letters D-i-n-k-y under his bonnet
could be an ancient registration mark
that might explain his size.

I love his little hub caps!
I gently prise off each one to clean between his spokes.
He's so perfect, not a mark anywhere,
not a single rough patch
and the best news yet –
his Pre-rust Susceptibility scrape is negative.
I'm suffering from the Post-reproduction exhausts,
Li's too fast for me. If I can't keep up with him now,
how am I going to manage when he's completely run in?

The archivists say Li's kind was sacred in Earth time.
Many households built special temples which were used as
shrines. Soapy ablutions, waxings and polishings were
ritually performed. The worshippers considered this such
a special act of reverence that a certain time was
regularly set aside for those observances.

Entry 3   cosine 16

I've installed in Li's room the mandatory alarm system,
a bird clock programmed to give two calls:
one when his fatty acids require draining,
the other when he needs refueling.
Automatically all Li's exhaust emissions are recycled
or would be if I ever put Li in his detox suite.
Of course I don't, I'm against supermechanisms
and I will not have Li objectified.
I keep him with me (day) and us (night).
Orwen doesn't like that last bit,
but, as I explain, Li's so small,
when he grows it'll be different.
My old-fashioned way of bringing up Li is
[and I do hate to admit it] part of the problem.
It is labour-intensive, so at night
I'm too tired to entangle with Orwen.
He screeches, calls me a ding-a-ling, a riderless horse,
a danger to myself and every one around me.
He says that it has taken aeons of time,
dark ages spent in black holes as anti-matter,
to develop all the technology that I am NOT using.
What has he done to deserve a naïve, twisted primitive?
He'd have me know that one deadly virus
from my crackpot ideas could wreck the whole system.
Guilt softens me. Spineless and silent
I become as malleable as fuse wire.

Entry 4   cosine 18

At last, I've learned better than to answer Orwen
when he's philosophical. Instead I let myself loosen.
As I watch the copper hairs around his mouth
twitch with emotion, I can't keep away from him.
Deep in my rib cage, precious bits of me that were
fossilized ferns unfurl and tremble with life.
I can touch and feel Orwen with a sixth sense
which is twice the sum of them all.
When we unravel, it is each into his own
unique and untwisted wiriness.
Afterwards, in the smoothness of furling
Orwen will whisper, in French: O equal Zero.

Then I tell him that I can see, smell and hear
for myself what Li needs and that's good enough.
And yes, I am going to keep Li with us at night.

Entry 5   cosine 20

Li's favorite toy is an old gas meter
from Orwen's collection of early measuring instruments,
[source material for his thesis
Early Man's Obsession with the Commodity]. He wanted
to explore the idea that quality can be quantified
with financial exchange. He was disqualified –
the adjudicators said the subject was obscene.
Orwen can be touchingly innocent sometimes.
Now we have to scrape by with the little we get
from the students who come to study his collection.
Just enough for the anti-rust clinic and,
thanks to them, our degeneration is slowing down.
Li's so little, he is going to need us both
until he grows up. Though as Orwen says:
What has wheels moves on
and size doesn't come into the equation.

He's glad that Li has fun with the gas meter.
Better than some academic making use of it
to mount his favourite hobby horse.
Owen will always bring a horse into the conversation.
In Earth time, he was the groom in charge
of the Lipizzaner stud farm and
he's never going to forget it.
He thinks horses are sacred,
tells me it is poetry that Li is making
when he spins the two brass cog wheels of the greasy meter.
As they run round connecting and interconnecting,
Li and Orwen imitate the sounds which they think they hear,
whinny, snort and snuffle, happy in their world of tongues.

Li has discovered a meadow, where he likes to play.
It lies between the two rivers, Noumena and Phenomena.
He tunnels in the hard sand and has unearthed
a set of twelve spoons with male heads.
The Brain Machine has identified them as apostles.
Li amuses himself arranging them in circles
or lying one inside the other.
Orwen has now decided he is ready to have
his own set of 26 hieroglyphs.
He wants to teach him prepositions.
Their function, or so Orwen says, is like that of cog wheels.
Father and son group and regroup their ins and outs,
their if and buts. Sometimes Li will make
a circle of spoons, then Orwen will put the hieroglyph
INSIDE at the centre and the hieroglyph OUTSIDE
by itself and far away from the circle.
He carefully explains
that much further back
than his memory can clearly go,
these positions were important.
Your life could be at risk if you didn't know the answer
when asked, to the questions
Friend or Foe?
Insider or Outsider?

Entry 7   cosine 24 [2 lines re placement of dashes]

Today, Orwen told Li the story of the goddess Silver Cloud.
He said she was so beautiful everyone who saw her
desired to possess her. She spoke softly;
the sound of her words reassured all who heard them.
Orwen didn't get any further for suddenly he seized up.
It was as though someone had poured superglue all over him.
Both Li and I were frightened, though Li is much quicker
than I am to recover himself in a crisis.
Quickly he lubricated Orwen with his 3-in-1 medication,
carefully rubbing in the excess. He is meticulous.
His size makes him nimble and he's such a practical boy.
Sometimes I worry that he is lumbered with us –
a couple of old crocks for parents. But not for long,
we three have too much fun together,
I can't stay with gloomy thoughts. However,
I did insist that Orwen goes to the corrosion specialist.
Li spent the rest of the evening writing ditties to amuse us -
these are the only two I can remember –

Two little centimetres sitting on a ruler
when they were inches
then they were cooler.

Along came a great big metre, not at all flustered
said his system was
hotter than mustard.

Entry 8   cosine 26

Here I am with Orwen and Li.
I, Noemi, who does not give
a rusty spigot for sequence
or cadence, listening
to the two of them
figuring out logistics.
What in a world of twisted wire
and corrosion is that?
Orwen says it's the study of words,
their rules and regulations -
the tension of tenses.
Most of all, he emphasizes,
 it's about how to live in time,
 or in his case, because he's understood
 how everything slips so easily
 into its opposite,
 how not to live in Corrosion Time.
I MUST stop asking:
In time to what?

Entry 9 cosine 28

I am still irritating Orwen
by asking stupid questions.
Today again, I asked:
In time to what?
I do hate to admit it,
but I am flattered
by [what some would call]
verbal abuse.
It's the attention,
the passion in his voice,
the power he assumes for me
when he screeches -
at the top of his twist:
You corroded bimbo,
even you, Noemi, must have heard
of LIFETIME, Life/time.
I know though that they write the answers
before the questions.
So, if you ask a question of logistics,
you get an answer, sure enough,
but it doesn't answer your question.
Orwen and Li hide behind the word
when they want to gang up on me.
They do it so naturally, because they have
that one extra twist of wire
which I do not.
All this unraveling of twisted wire,
to understand that which – for good
or bad – I take for granted.

I woke this morning with an attack of the horrors,
the screaming hab-dabs. I hadn't slept
and was conscious of a knot of hatred – not undirected
but object-specific. I had woken up with a hatred
for that of which I am made – METAL –
the very substance of my being.
I hated the way the upper half of my body stuck out,
the obscene thickness around my middle
and most of all the pimples and dents of my surface.
Abhorrent to myself, I vowed to disintegrate
and never again visit the Rust Clinic or the Brain Machine
and above all not to say anything to Orwen.
Now I had an irrational hatred
to set against all that was rational,
or that had presented as rational in my life.
Better to disintegrate than be stabilized
into a condition of total predictability.
In the night, I had seen a vision of a human pin-cushion,
except the pins were knives. He spoke to me,
said he was called Sebastian and that many humans,
in the past, had thought like me. They had a word for it,
it was Mortification and, in his case,
Mortification of the Flesh.

Entry 11 cosine 32

Orwen is too keen to instruct Li in Corrosion Process.
It is hard to watch, especially as I don't see the point.
Time and rusting are best not explained to the very young.
I wish Orwen would let Li find out for himself,
treat him as he does me, answer when asked otherwise keep
his knowledge to himself. Who knows the length of wire
that is needed to make me or Orwen or Li?
For Orwen the study of length of life and time go back
to his research on early measuring machines.
He hasn't managed to let go of all that
because he put too much of himself into it.
Li's mind is cluttered with all that stuff.
It will take him so long to unlearn.
Some things are best left to the imagination,
spelling things out correctly
[or what Orwen sees as correctly] can stultify a young mind.

Entry 12   cosine 34

Each morning I rub off any rust
that has formed on me and little Li,
Orwen does the same for himself.
We each have a jar to put it in.
My jar is labeled Noemi Metal,
Life Debris with the date of collection.
When the jar is full, it is taken
for assessment to the Rust Clinic.
In ancient earth time,
the Brain Machine says six sounds
were given to the overall report
constructed from their findings,

au – to – bi – og – gra – phy.

Finis

www.ingramcontent.com/pod-product-compliance
Lightning Source LLC
Chambersburg PA
CBHW020954030426
42339CB00004B/98